THE Jane Austen COMPANION TO Life

sourcebooks

Published by Sourcebooks, Inc.
P.O. Box 4410, Naperville, Illinois 60567-4410
(630) 961-3900
Fax: (630) 961-2168
www.sourcebooks.com

Printed and bound in China.
OGP 10 9 8 7 6 5 4 3 2

About the Illustrations and Font

* * *

Illustrators Charles Edmund Brock and his brother, Henry Matthew Brock, provided illustrations for many of the most popular books published on the cusp of the twentieth century. C. E. Brock completed illustrations for *Pride and Prejudice* in 1895, *Sense and Sensibility* in 1906, and various illustrations for *Emma*, *Northanger Abbey*, *Mansfield Park*, and *Persuasion* in 1907 and 1908. Both Charles and Henry illustrated for the six novels in the 1906 anthology *The Novels and Letters of Jane Austen* (Manor House Edition, edited by R. Brimley Jonnson). The two brothers shared a studio and were sources of great inspiration to one another.

The title font and where it appears internally throughout, aptly named "Jane Austen," is based on Austen's actual handwriting.

Introduction

• • •

On December 16, 1775, Jane Austen, one of the world's greatest novelists, was born. She was the seventh child born to Reverend George Austen and his wife, Cassandra. Having produced only six novels, she is nonetheless regarded as one of the most popular authors ever to come from England. Her novels, letters, and minor works have both touched the hearts of casual readers and exercised the brains of scholars. She is at the same time accessible and untouchable, and she has inspired a veritable industry of sequels, adaptations, movies, and miniseries.

On these pages you will find Jane's most honest thoughts on life, from the practical to the lighthearted to the philosophic. Let her advice guide you to find happiness and contentment, just as the heroines in her novels always do.

EMMA

"How do you like my gown?"

"One cannot have too large a party."

—Mr. Weston in *Emma*

"Oh God! her father and mother!"

"If things are going untowardly one month, they are sure to mend the next."

—Mr. Weston in *Emma*

"The enjoyment of Elinor's company"

On Character

"Wisdom is better than wit, and in the long run will certainly have the laugh on her side."

—from a letter to her niece, Fanny Knight

"Make haste! Make haste!"

*"Angry people are
not always wise."*

—from *Pride and Prejudice*

"'Hum,' said Mrs Ferrars, 'very pretty'"

"One man's style must not be the rule of another's."

—Mr. Weston in *Emma*

"The kitchen-garden was to be next admired"

On Character

"It is well to have as many holds upon happiness as possible."

—Henry Tilney in *Northanger Abbey*

"And this offer of marriage you have refused?"

"Your affection gives me the highest pleasure, but indeed you must not let anything depend on my opinion; your own feelings, and none but your own, should determine such an important point."

—from a letter to her niece, Fanny Knight, on whether Fanny should accept a marriage proposal

"He could not help giving Mrs Norris a hint"

On Human Nature

"We have all a better guide in ourselves, if we would attend to it, than any other person can be."

—Fanny Price in *Mansfield Park*

"We have brought you some strangers"

*"Silly things do cease to be silly
if they are done by sensible people in
an impudent way. Wickedness is always
wickedness, but folly is not always
folly. It depends upon the character
of those who handle it."*

—Emma Woodhouse in *Emma*

"Well done, Miss Anne!"

*"My idea of good company
is the company of clever,
well-informed people who have
a great deal of conversation;
that is what I call good company."*

—Anne Elliot in *Persuasion*

"Standing together over the hearth"

On Human Nature

"Nothing is more deceitful than the appearance of humility. It is often only carelessness of opinion, and sometimes an indirect boast."

—Mr. Darcy in *Pride and Prejudice*

"Henry drove so well"

"There is nothing like employment, active indispensable employment, for relieving sorrow."

—from *Mansfield Park*

Emma

"'You are extremely kind,' replied Miss Bates"

On Character

"Respect for right conduct is felt by everybody."

—Mr. Knightley in *Emma*

"In earnest contemplation"

"Vanity and pride are different things, though the words are often used synonymously. A person may be proud without being vain. Pride relates more to our opinion of ourselves; vanity, to what we would have others think of us."

—Mary Bennet in *Pride and Prejudice*

EMMA

"Most beloved Emma—tell me at once"

On Human Nature

. . .

"Seldom, very seldom, does complete truth belong to any human disclosure; seldom can it happen that something is not a little disguised, or a little mistaken."

—from *Emma*

"With a letter in her outstretched hand"

"I have now attained the true art of letter-writing, which we are always told, is to express on paper exactly what one would say to the same person by word of mouth."

—from a letter to her sister Cassandra

MANSFIELD PARK

"He…left them only at the door"

On Character

"Selfishness must always be forgiven you know, because there is no hope of a cure."

—Mary Crawford in *Mansfield Park*

"He then sat down by her"

"Do not speak ill of your sense merely for the gratification of your fancy; yours is sense which deserves more honourable treatment."

—from a letter to her niece,
Fanny Knight

"Of all the consequence in their power"

On Human Nature

"There are people, who the more you do for them, the less they will do for themselves."

—from *Emma*

"Complete in his lieutenant's uniform"

"There is nothing like staying at home for real comfort."

—Mrs. Elton in *Emma*

"You must allow me to present this young lady to you"

On Character

• • •

"Those who do not complain are never pitied."

—Mrs. Bennet in *Pride and Prejudice*

EMMA

"Begged them not to want more, or to use her ill"

"What is right to be done cannot be done too soon."

—Mr. Churchill in *Emma*

"She very soon heard Captain Wentworth and Louisa"

On Human Nature

"What wild imaginations one forms where dear self is concerned! How sure to be mistaken!"

—Anne Elliot in *Persuasion*

"She was forced to listen"

*"Where an opinion is general,
it is usually correct."*

—Mary Crawford in *Mansfield Park*

PERSUASION

"With eyes of glowing entreaty fixed on her"

On Human Nature

• • •

"One man's ways may be as good as another's, but we all like our own best."

—Admiral Croft in *Persuasion*

"'Read it aloud,' said their father"

"I had a very pleasant evening, however, though you will probably find out that there was no particular reason for it; but I do not think it worthwhile to wait for enjoyment until there is some real opportunity for it."

—from a letter to her sister Cassandra

"Colonel Brandon was invited to visit her"

On Character

"There is something so amiable in the prejudices of a young mind, that one is sorry to see them give way to the reception of more general opinions."

—Colonel Brandon in *Sense and Sensibility*

"In vain were the well-meant condescensions of Sir Thomas"

"The person, be it gentleman or lady, who has not pleasure in a good novel, must be intolerably stupid."

—Henry Tilney in *Northanger Abbey*

MANSFIELD PARK

"Dr Grant himself went out with an umbrella"